This Workbook Belongs To _____

Student Workbook
Animal Farm
Critical Thinking Through Literature

Study Questions

Vocabulary Study

Elements of Fiction

Writing Assignments

Activities

Based On
The Book By
Geroge Orwell

Use this workbook to get the most out of your reading.
Answer questions completely and thoughtfully.

COPYRIGHT INFORMATION

This is copyrighted material.
The purchaser may print or copy the student materials
for his or her classroom use only.
Do not post these mateials to the Internet.

Copyright violations are prosecuted to the fullest extent of the law
and are subject to a minimum of a $500.00 fine,
imposed by the publisher,
in addition to any other legal judgments obtained.

Cover Image: ID 43136704 © Gstockstudio1 | Dreamstime.com

ISBN 978-1-60249-714-6

Copyright 2015

Mary B. Collins

Table of Contents

Animal Farm

Student Workbook

5	Overview Calendar
6	About the Author George Orwell
7	Reading Assignment Sheet
8	Research Project
9	Vocabulary RA 1 Chapters 1-3
15	Study Questions RA 1 Chapters 1-3
18	About Oral Reading
19	Vocabulary RA 2 Chapters 4-6
23	Study Questions RA 2 Chapters 4-6
26	Vocabulary RA 3 Chapters 7-8
30	Study Questions RA 3 Chapters 7-8
34	Writing Assignment 1
35	Rules, Contracts, Truth, and Lies
37	Vocabulary RA 4 Chapters 9-10
41	Study Questions RA 4 Chapters 9-10
43	Equality, Individuality, and Civilization
45	Use of Propaganda in Animal Farm
47	Steps By Which Pigs Become Human
49	Revision of the Commandments
51	Snowball's Fall From Honor
53	Man's Inhumanity to Man
55	Passages From Animal Farm
57	Elements of Fiction: Character Traits
58	Elements of Fiction: Conflict Chart
59	Elements of Fiction: Plot Diagram
60	Crossword 1
62	Crossword 2
64	Vocabulary Crossword 1
65	Vocabulary Crossword 2

Animal Farm Notes

OVERVIEW - CALENDAR VIEW
Animal Farm

1 Background Project Assignment	2 Research Pre-reading RA#1	3 Oral Reading RA#1	4 Quiz RA #1 Study ?s RA#1 Preview RA#2	5 Vocab RA #2 Minilesson: Persuasion & Control Read RA #2
6 Quiz RA#2 Study ?s RA#2 Preview RA#3	7 Vocab RA #3 Writing Assignment Read RA#3	8 Minilesson: Rules, Contracts, Truth, and Lies	9 Quiz RA #3 Study ?s RA #3 Preview RA#4	10 Vocab RA#4 Minilesson: Equality, Individualism & Civilization Read RA#4
11 Quiz RA#4 Study ?s RA#4	12 Group Discussion of Topics	13 Analyze Passages	14 Minilessons: Characterization, Conflict, Plot, & Symbolism	15 Reading Skills, Language Use, & Ideas
16 Vocabulary Review	17 Unit Review	18 Unit Test		

A FEW NOTES ABOUT THE AUTHOR
George Orwell

ORWELL, George (1903-50). As a journalist and writer of autobiographical narratives, George Orwell was outstanding. But he will be remembered primarily for two works of fiction that have become 20th-century classics: *Animal Farm*, published in 1944, and *Nineteen Eighty-Four* (l949).

George Orwell is a pen name. His real name was Eric Arthur Blair, and he was born in 1903 at Montihari in Bengal, India, where his father was a minor British official. His family had social status but little money, a fact that influenced Orwell's later attitude toward the English class system and the empire's treatment of its subject peoples. About 1911 the family returned to England. Blair was sent to school in Sussex, where he was distinguished both by his poverty and his intelligence. He later wrote of his miserable school years in *Such, Such Were the Joys* (1953). He attended Eton in the years 1917 to 1921 but decided against going on to a university. Instead he went to Burma as a member of the British imperial police.

His own poverty, plus his growing aversion to Britain's imperial policies, led him to resign from the government in 1928 and spend several years as a vagrant among the poor and outcast of Europe. He also spent time among the unemployed miners in the north of England. These experiences were recounted in *Down and Out in Paris and London* (1933) and *The Road to Wigan Pier* (1937). Then Orwell was off to Spain to report on the Civil War. His adventures in Spain were told in *Homage to Catalonia* (1938), one of his best books.

During World War II Orwell wrote for the British Broadcasting Company and worked as a literary editor for the London Tribune. Publication of *Animal Farm* in 1944 made him rich at long last, and he could devote himself to writing. He bought a house on the island of Jura, where he wrote *Nineteen Eighty-Four*. By the time it was published, Orwell was already ill from tuberculosis--from which he died on Jan. 21, 1950, in London.

--- Courtesy of Compton's Learning Company

READING ASSIGNMENT SHEET
Animal Farm

Assignment	Chapters	Read By Date
Reading Assignment 1	1-3	
Reading Assignment 2	4-6	
Reading Assignment 3	7-8	
Reading Assignment 4	9-10	

Any page numbers given herein reference the Signet Classic text, ISBN: 978-0-451-52634-2.

RESEARCH PROJECT DIRECTIONS
Animal Farm

Purposes

- To be able to better understand and appreciate the book *Animal Farm*, you need to have some background information about a variety of topics: the Russian Revolution, Stalin, Russia's role in WWII, George Orwell, and the literary terms *allegory* and *fable*. Your group has been assigned to find out about one of these topics.
- This assignment is being made not only to prepare you for getting the most out of *Animal Farm*, but also to take the opportunity to practice a variety of skills that you will need in life: working with others, finding and understanding information from a variety of sources, and communicating the information you find to others, in both spoken and written forms.
- In addition, the information you learn will not only help you better understand *Animal Farm*; it will help you become an educated person, one who has a broad base of knowledge to draw from in evaluating, participating in, and succeeding in real life situations.

Process

- Each of the topics in this assignment has had volumes written about it and, in many cases, movies or documentary films created to tell about it. With *so much* and such *detailed* information available, part of the challenge of this assignment is to find sources that give an overview of the topic in enough detail to give the information you need–but not in so much detail that you get bogged down in minutia.
- The first steps to take are:
    1. All of you in the group should find out what information sources are available.
    2. Determine which sources are reliable and suit the purposes of this assignment.
    3. Decide who in the group will read, watch, or otherwise get information from each source you choose.
    4. Each of you get information from your assigned sources.
- After you all have your information, get back together as a group to tell each other what you have found out.
    1. As you share information, make a list of the most important points that are brought up in your discussion.
    2. Then, go through your list and hone it to include the facts that you believe are the most important to share with the class. Make enough copies of your list for everyone.

- When all the group work is completed, we will come back together as a class to share and discuss the information everyone has gathered on the various topics. Everyone in the class will have copies of all the fact lists for reference and study purposes.

Follow-Up
- To assess how much of the information you absorbed about the topics, and to help put that information into your longer term memory, you will be asked to give a written answer to one broad question about each topic. Answer each question thoroughly in your best, standard, written English.
- If you find any of these topics particularly interesting, follow-up with watching more videos or reading more about the topic(s) of interest.

Conclusion
- As with most things in life, you will get out of this assignment what you put into it. If you approach it with some energy, curiosity, and diligence, you will learn things an educated person should know, practice skills that will serve you well through life, and gain knowledge that will help to make understanding *Animal Farm* a little easier.
- As you read *Animal Farm*, these various pieces will fall into place. After you finish reading the book, we will focus on exploring the ideas and themes presented in the book in light of its historical context and this background information.

RESEARCH PROJECT FOLLOW-UP
Writing Assignment 1 - *Animal Farm*

Purpose:

By doing this writing assignment, you will synthesize the materials covered in class. You will have to review your notes and think about the most important elements of each topic, then find your own words to explain each item. This increases your understanding and helps to put the information in longer-term memory for use later. This assignment also helps you practice logical thinking and word selection, as well as communicating and writing skills. The directions are simple, and the task is not very difficult, but you use, develop, and reinforce a lot of behind-the-scenes skills to accomplish it.

As a follow-up to the research project the class did, answer each of the following questions thoroughly and completely based on the class discussions, your notes, and your own thoughts. Each answer should be at least one well-written, complete paragraph including a topic sentence.

1. What was the Russian Revolution?
2. Who was Joseph Stalin?
3. What role did Russia play in World War II?
4. Who was George Orwell?
5. Explain what an allegory is.
6. Explain what a fable is.

VOCABULARY: READING ASSIGNMENT 1
Animal Farm Chapters 1-3

PART I: Using Prior Knowledge And Contextual Clues
Use any clues you can find in the sentences from the text combined with your prior knowledge and write what you think the bold word means.

1. He seldom talked, and when he did, it was usually to make some **cynical** remark--for instance, he would say that God had given him a tail to keep the flies off, but that he would sooner have had no tail and no flies.

2. Is it not crystal clear, then, comrades, that all the evils of this life of ours spring from the **tyranny** of human beings?

3. And remember, comrades, your resolution must never **falter**.

4. **Pre-eminent** among the pigs were two young boars named Snowball and Napoleon, whom Mr. Jones was breeding up for sale.

5. Snowball was a more **vivacious** pig than Napoleon, quicker in speech and more inventive, but was not considered to have the same depth of character.

6. At the beginning they met with much stupidity and **apathy**.

7. He did his work in the same slow **obstinate** way as he had done it in Jones's time, never shirking and never volunteering for extra work either.

Animal Farm Vocabulary: Reading Assignment 1 Page 2

8. Snowball also busied himself with organising the other animals into what he called Animal Committees. He was **indefatigable** at this.

PART II: Matching
Considering the usage in Part I, match the vocabulary words to their definitions.

____ 1. cynical   A. Stubbornly inflexible

____ 2. tyranny   B. Untiring; tireless

____ 3. falter   C. Lack of interest or emotion

____ 4. preeminent   D. Lively; spirited

____ 5. vivacious   E. Outstanding

____ 6. apathy   F. Bitterly mocking

____ 7. obstinate   G. Hesitate; fail; waver

____ 8. indefatigable   H. Absolute power, especially power used unjustly

Part III: Cloze Passage
Fill in the blanks with the appropriate vocabulary words from the list above.

The _____ campaign manager expressed a very _____ remark concerning what he felt was the _____ shown by the candidate for office toward his staff. He did not _____ in saying exactly what he meant about the _____ politician who could not take any advice from his hardworking, _____ employees. They who had begun their work for him with such a _____ spirit, full of excitement, now felt nothing but _____ towards the campaign.

PART IV: Words In Practice
Answer the questions and be able to give short explanations to justify your answers.

1. Is a person who is **cynical** likely to be moved by an idealistic speech?

2. If a boss is **tyrannical**, is she mild-mannered or demanding?

3. The audience gasped as the highwire artist faltered. Why would his **faltering** cause the audience to gasp?

4. Does a **preeminent** person deserve some amount of respect? Why?

5. Who would we expect to be more **vivacious**--an office worker or an extreme sports enthusiast?

6. The whole senior class was **apathetic** after returning from spring break. Were they enthusiastic about getting back into the school routine, or were they acting like they wished they were still on vacation?

7. What is the best way to get an **obstinate** toddler to comply with what you want her to do?

8. Give an example of someone who could be considered **indefatigable**.

Animal Farm Vocabulary: Reading Assignment 1 Page 4

PART V: Other Word Forms
Below are some other forms of some of the words from Reading Assignment 1.

cynical	cynic
tyranny	tyrant; tyrannical
falter	faltered; faltering; falters
preeminent	preeminently
vivacious	vivaciously; vivaciousness
apathy	apathetic; apathetically
obstinate	obstinately; obstinateness
indefatigable	indefatigably

PART VI: Usage

Write a little story in which you use one form of each of your vocabulary words from Assignment 1.

STUDY QUESTIONS READING ASSIGNMENT 1
Animal Farm Chapters 1-3

1. *Animal Farm* is a type of fiction called an *allegorical fable*, in which animals represent people and ideas in order to teach a lesson. What does this tell you about the content of the book?

2. In a fable, animals represent types of people. What do the pigs, the horses, and the sheep represent in the first three chapters of *Animal Farm*?

3. What is the central conflict outlined in Old Major's speech to the animals? What might this represent in the world at large?

4. Why does Old Major tell the animals to avoid living in a house, wearing clothes, or otherwise taking on the habits of humanity?

5. Why is it important for the animals to have their own anthem and flag?

6. What troubles do the founders of Animalism face in getting their beliefs across to other animals? What helped Animalism along?

7. Could Mr. Jones have done anything to prevent the rebellion? Use facts from the book to support your answer.

8. Why is it significant that Boxer burns his straw hat?

9. After Mr. Jones is chased off of the farm, describe how the pigs take charge.

10. The pigs are described in chapter three as natural leaders. Do you think this is so? Why or why not?

11. What is the purpose of the maxim "four legs good, two legs bad?"

12. Some minor characters in the novel represent larger segments of a population. Who could Moses, Mollie, Clover, and Benjamin represent?

Animal Farm Study Questions Reading Assignment 1 Page 3

13. At the end of Chapter II, Napoleon tells the animals to "never mind the milk...That will be attended to." And at the end of Chapter III, Squealer is sent out to explain why the pigs need the milk and apples. The animals thought these would be shared equally among all the animals, and yet they go along with Squealer's explanation. Why?

14. By the end of the third chapter things seem to be going very well for the animals. What foreshadowing do you see that indicates things will take a turn for the worse?

15. Identify
    A. Beasts of England

    B. The Seven Commandments

    C. Sugarcandy Mountain

ABOUT ORAL READING

Oral reading is something most people have to do at some point in their lives. Here is a list of a few times when you might want to be able to have good oral reading skills:

- giving a report in front of classmates at school or colleagues at work
- making a presentation to prospective customers or clients
- reading story books to your siblings or your own children at home
- making a speech or toast at a wedding
- giving a eulogy for a loved one
- sharing a funny story or an article from a book, paper, or the Internet with a friend

The best way to improve your oral reading is to do it frequently. If the only time you read orally is in class, you are not likely to improve quickly. Here are some tips about how to improve your oral reading:

Practice. Read aloud to yourself at home. Read the cereal box in the morning, posts your friends have made on your media page, text messages friends send to you, recipes, instructions, news articles, comic book or graphic novel bubbles...anything that has printed words.

Pre-read. Before you begin reading something orally, read it silently first. Because you are familiar with the text from reading it silently once, your oral reading will go better.

Reread. It sounds silly and obvious, but it works. Read aloud something you have read aloud before, or repeat reading the same sentence(s) more than once. Each time you repeat a sentence, it gets easier to read because you are more familiar with it. Your mouth works better because your mind knows what's coming. Each time you read the same sentence over again, try for smoother fluency and more expression.

Pretend. Imagine you are in a situation that requires better projection or clearer enunciation. You are a king or queen making a proclamation to the subjects of your kingdom gathered in your courtyard. You are in a room of old people who are hard of hearing. You're delivering a special message to a friend and want to say it perfectly. The possibilities are endless...and helpful.

Ask For Feedback. Read with a friend, each practicing your oral reading, then evaluate each other. Read to a parent, guardian, or relative and ask how you did. Repeat the process often.

Mind Reading. Read to yourself in your mind. Listen for your outwardly silent, inner voice as you read the words on the page.

The more you read, the better you'll get!

VOCABULARY: READING ASSIGNMENT 2
Animal Farm Chapters 4-6

PART I: Using Prior Knowledge And Contextual Clues
Use any clues you can find in the sentences from the text combined with your prior knowledge and write what you think the bold word means.

1. Its owner was a Mr. Frederick, a tough, **shrewd** man, **perpetually** involved in lawsuits and with a name for driving a hard bargain.

2. And yet the song was **irrepressible**.

3. And so within five minutes of their invasion they were in **ignominious** retreat by the same way as they had come, with a flock of geese hissing after them and pecking at their calves all the way.

4. An **impromptu** celebration of the victory was held immediately.

5. There was also "Animal Hero, Second Class," which was conferred **posthumously** on the dead sheep.

6. It was noticed that they were especially liable to break into "Four legs good, two legs bad" at **crucial** moments in Snowball's speeches.

7. But of all their **controversies**, none was so bitter as the one that took place over the windmill.

8. On every **pretext** she would run away from work and go to the drinking pool, where she would stand foolishly gazing at her own reflection in the water.

Animal Farm Vocabulary: Reading Assignment 2 Page 2

PART II: Matching
Considering the usage in Part I, match the vocabulary words to their definitions.

____ 1. shrewd   A. excuse

____ 2. perpetually   B. critical; of supreme importance

____ 3. irrepressible C. disputes

____ 4. ignominious   D. astute; clever

____ 5. impromptu   E. disgraceful; shameful

____ 6. posthumously   F. impossible to control or restrain

____ 7. pretext   G. not rehearsed; at the spur of the moment

____ 8. crucial   H. continually

____ 9. controversies I. after one's death

Part III: Cloze Passage
Fill in the blanks with the appropriate vocabulary words from the list above. You may need to use different forms of the words.

The son of a prominent businessman approached the Board of Directors of his father's business on the _____ of securing the _____ success of the company. In a _____ manner he shared many _____ facts and _____ that had been part of his father's business dealings, leaving out _____ information that would have shed a better light on the whole subject. He was _____ in conveying his disdain of how his father had ruined the business. As the meeting was coming to an end, a message was sent to the boardroom stating that his father had suddenly died that afternoon. An _____ decision was made to _____ award his father with the company's highest honors.

Animal Farm Vocabulary: Reading Assignment 2 Page 3

PART IV: Words In Practice
Answer the questions and be able to give short explanations to justify your answers.

1. When making an important financial decision, would you want an advisor who is shrewd?

2. If you were in perpetual motion all day long, would you be very tired at the end of the day?

3. Is a child with irrepressible energy easy to control?

4. Should someone with an ignominious reputation be admired or shunned?

5. What is one good example of an impromptu action?

6. Sometimes authors have works published posthumously. Are they likely to benefit personally from the sales of their posthumously published books?

7. Give an example of a crucial moment in American or world history.

8. What are some controversies in current events this year?

9. If your mother comes into your room under the pretext of returning clean laundry to see what you are doing on your computer would you be upset? Why or why not?

PART V:
Below are some other forms of the vocabulary words from Reading Assignment #2.

shrewd shrewdly; shrewdness
perpetually perpetual
irrepressible irrepressibly; irrepressibleness; irrepressibility
ignominious ignominiously; ignominiousness
impromptu
posthumously posthumous
pretext pretexts
crucial cruciality; crucially
controversies controversy; controversial; controversially

PART VI: Usage
Write a little story in which you use one form of each of your vocabulary words from Assignment 2.

STUDY QUESTIONS READING ASSIGNMENT 2
Animal Farm Chapters 4-6

1. Why are the other human farm owners so upset by the rebellion at Animal Farm?

2. During the Battle of the Cowshed, Boxer strikes a human on the head with his hoof. What does his reaction to the thought that the young man is dead tell you about his character?

3. What do the events of the Battle of the Cowshed tell you about Snowball's character?

4. Snowball tells all the animals that they should be ready to die for Animal Farm if need be. What do you think of this style of political rhetoric? Would you trust a leader who uses it?

5. Mollie the mare runs away from Animal Farm to work for humans again. Why does she do this?

6. Describe the debate styles favored by Napoleon and Snowball. Which do you prefer?

Animal Farm Study Questions Chapters 4-6 Page 2

7. Describe the character of Benjamin the donkey. What do you think of his attitude toward life?

8. Napoleon sics dogs on Snowball, chasing him off of the farm, after Snowball speaks passionately about the windmill. Why do you think he waited until that moment?

9. Why is it important that the dogs wagged their tails to Napoleon in the same way as the other dogs used to do to Mr. Jones?

10. How does Napoleon convince the animals that it is right for him to cancel all Sunday meetings and votes?

11. It is revealed that Napoleon is actually in favor of the windmill. Did this surprise you when you read it? Why does Napoleon change his mind?

Animal Farm Study Questions Chapters 4-6 Page 3

12. The work the animals must do under Napoleon is extremely difficult. It comes out that they can volunteer to work on Sundays, but if they do not volunteer, they will receive half rations. Why do you think their choice is presented this way?

13. It is discovered that there are items required that cannot function on the farm, and so Napoleon decides that they must engage in trade. Do you think this is a wise choice for the farm? Why or why not?

14. Many of the animals are resistant to the idea of engaging in trade, based on the statements of Major. What does Squealer say that calms them?

15. One of the rules of Animalism changes from "No Animal Shall Sleep In A Bed" to "No Animal Shall Sleep In A Bed *With Sheets*." Why does this change? What does this change indicate for the future of Animal Farm?

16. The destruction of the windmill is blamed on Snowball. Why would Napoleon want the animals to think that Snowball is so powerful?

VOCABULARY: READING ASSIGNMENT 3
Animal Farm Chapters 7-8

PART I: Using Prior Knowledge And Contextual Clues
Use any clues you can find in the sentences from the text combined with your prior knowledge and write what you think the bold word means.

1. **Emboldened** by the collapse of the windmill, the human beings were inventing fresh lies about Animal Farm.

2. For five days the hens held out, then they **capitulated** and went back to their nesting boxes.

3. "For we have reason to think that some of Snowball's secret agents are **lurking** among us at this moment!"

4. Napoleon appeared to change **countenance**, and sharply ordered Boxer to let the dog go....

5. Presently the **tumult** died down.

6. When he did appear, he was attended not only by his **retinue** of dogs but by a black cockerel who marched in front of him and acted as a kind of trumpeter . . . .

7. As the summer wore on, and the windmill neared completion, the rumors of an **impending** treacherous attack grew stronger and stronger.

8. In addition, four pigeons were sent to Foxwood with a **conciliatory** message, which it was hoped might re-establish good relations with Pilkington.

PART II: Matching
Considering the usage in Part I, match the vocabulary words to their definitions.

____ 1. emboldened   A. those accompanying a person of rank

____ 2. capitulated   B. showing good-will; peace-making

____ 3. countenance   C. encouraged; made brave

____ 4. lurking   D. about to take place

____ 5. tumult   E. gave up all resistance

____ 6. retinue   F. exist concealed or unsuspected

____ 7. conciliatory   G. facial expression

____ 8. impending   H. commotion

Part III: Cloze Passage
Fill in the blanks with the appropriate vocabulary words from the list above. You may need to use different forms of the words.

The photographer was _____ behind a hedge _____ by the possibility of getting a candid photograph of the celebrity who was about to arrive. As the celebrity approached with her _____, the _____ encounter only enhanced the nervous smile on the photographer's _____. Suddenly he leapt out from where he was hiding, and an immediate _____ ensued, created by the staff trying to whisk away their boss. Finally the celebrity _____, deciding it was easier to accommodate the photographer than trying to run away. In a _____ manner the photographer thanked the celebrity for her patience and good will.

Animal Farm Vocabulary: Reading Assignment 3 Page 3

PART IV: Words In Practice
Answer the questions and be able to give short explanations to justify your answers.

1. What might embolden a person to do something he or she would not normally do?

2. If the enemy capitulates, is the war over or is it still going on?

3. What kind of a person might be lurking outside your home?

4. What could you do to change your countenance?

5. Give en example of tumultuous weather.

6. Name someone who might have a retinue accompanying him or her.

7. Which thing could be impending, a scarf or a meeting?

8. If someone approaches you in a conciliatory manner, would you be afraid?

PART V:
Below are some other forms of the vocabulary words from Reading Assignment #3.

emboldened embolden; emboldens; emboldening
capitulated capitulate; capitulates; capitulating
lurking lurks; lurked; lurk
countenance countenances
tumult tumultuous
retinue
impending impend
conciliatory conciliate; conciliative; conciliating

PART VI: Usage
Write a little story in which you use one form of each of your vocabulary words from Assignment #3.

STUDY QUESTIONS READING ASSIGNMENT 3
Animal Farm Chapters 7-8

1. Why is it important that the animals rebuild the windmill with walls three feet thick?

2. Why do you think the animals find more comfort and inspiration in Boxer's "I will work harder!" than they do in Squealer's speeches?

3. Why, with starvation staring the animals in the face, is it "vitally necessary to conceal this fact from the outside world?"

4. What inspires the hens' rebellion? What does their treatment tell you about the pigs' respect for the tenets of Animalism?

5. Why does Napoleon keep waffling in between selling the wood to Pilkington or to Frederick?

Animal Farm Study Questions Chapters 7-8 Page 2

6. Compare and contrast the raven Moses's Sugarcandy Mountain with the spectre of Snowball haunting the farm.

7. Napoleon calls together the animals in the yard and sets his dogs on some of them, who he declares are traitors. Which animals are attacked first, and why?

8. The violence on Animal Farm escalates very quickly, going from strict rationing to brutal executions in just a few pages. Why does Orwell choose to portray it this way instead of continuing the slow build-up of oppression?

9. Discuss Clover's thoughts in the field after the executions.

10. Why is the singing of "Beasts of England" banned?

11. What are the implications behind the second changed commandment of Animalism?

12. All orders on Animal Farm are given though Squealer. How does Squealer change as time progresses in the story?

13. The animals state that they would rather have fewer figures and more food. Do you think the pigs are lying about their figures? Why would they lie about that?

14. Is the building of the windmill worth all the labor and difficulties the animals had to go through to get it?

Animal Farm Study Questions Chapters 7-8 Page 4

15. Compare and contrast the Battle of the Cowshed and the Battle of the Windmill.

16. When the windmill is destroyed, Squealer states confidently "We will build another windmill. We will build six windmills if we feel like it." Do you think this will be possible? Support your answer based on facts in the book.

WRITING ASSIGNMENT #1 - *Animal Farm*

PROMPT

In Chapter II The Seven Commandments for the animals are spelled out in no uncertain terms. Every society has certain rules that the members of that society must follow. There are many rules in our society that are written; law libraries are full of them. There are also some unwritten rules that guide our daily lives. (You shake hands when you meet someone new; you don't spit in someone else's soup; you say, "Excuse me" when you burp, etc.) Your assignment is to create a list of The Seven Commandments for our society. Choose the seven most basic and important rules (written or unwritten) that guide our lives. Defend your choices.

PREWRITING

Stop and think for a few minutes about what guidelines most people in our society follow. Jot down all your ideas. Then, go back and weed out those ideas that are duplicated or are not as important as some of the others on your list. Now, look at your list. If you were to give this list to a foreigner who had just arrived in this country, would these "commandments" serve him well? If not, go back and make revisions to your list until you are satisfied that you have the seven most basic rules of our society.

DRAFTING

Your paper should have an introductory paragraph in which you lead up to and state your seven commandments.

The body of your paper should have seven paragraphs: one for each commandment you have set forth. Your topic sentences for these paragraphs should set forth your commandments, and the body of your paragraphs should include your justifications for choosing the commandments.

Write a concluding paragraph in which you summarize your points and leave your reader with your most important thought.

PROMPT

When you finish the rough draft of your paper, ask a student who sits near you to read it. After reading your rough draft, he/she should tell you what he/she liked best about your work, which parts were difficult to understand, and ways in which your work could be improved. Reread your paper considering your critic's comments, and make the corrections you think are necessary.

PROOFREADING

Do a final proofreading of your paper double-checking your grammar, spelling, organization, and the clarity of your ideas.

RULES, CONTRACTS, TRUTH, and LIES
Animal Farm

One of the many reasons *Animal Farm* is considered a classic and is still being used in schools is that it is still relevant. Historical context aside, it speaks to the heart of civilization:

- It boldly and plainly shows us how one group gains power over and controls another group.
- It clearly paints accurate pictures of several basic types of individuals within a society.
- It shows the evolution of a society following revolution, based on the nature of mankind.

Those are all important things to recognize and study, but what do they mean for us?

One important theme that runs through all of these things is the role of rules, contracts, truth, and lies within a civilization. In class you have touched a bit on rules and contracts through discussions about the seven rules the animals set up on Animal Farm.

The rules are important, but the thing that is most important is the *evolution* of the rules: how the rules were changed without the input or knowledge of the working animals on the farm. The pigs changed them unilaterally and lied to the other animals, persuading them that the new rules had been the rules since the beginning. The old rules the animals remembered had never existed, the pigs said.

How do you know when you are being lied to? That's an important question for all of us in everyday life. The short answer is that you can't know something is a lie unless you know the truth. How can you be certain of the truth? Squealer's job of convincing the animals they were mistaken in their beliefs was made easier because the animals didn't have written copies of the original rules as proof that the rules on the fence had changed. He could lie to the animals and insert enough self-doubt in them that they rather quickly accepted the new rules as truth.

In daily life, that's what written contracts are for. Sales contracts, business agreements, licensing agreements, apartment leases and other kinds of contracts put down in black and white what each party involved agrees to so that as time passes we don't forget the original agreement and one side can't hoodwink (trick; deceive) the other side.

In a broader way, laws are contracts among all people in the society--written to put down in black and white the rules people in society agree to follow. Our representatives in the legislatures on the local, state, and national levels are supposed to agree upon and write down these laws. We, the people, elect folks to the legislature who are supposed to look out for our best interests in making these laws. Having many people debating the value of the laws, how they should be written, and whether or not they should be enacted protects us, the people, from having people like Napoleon and Squealer unilaterally deciding on the laws without consulting us (through our representatives). Giving the power of making laws to a large, representative group of people helps to keep one person from becoming a dictator, enacting only the laws he or she wants to make.

We trust that our representatives in the legislature will read, carefully consider, and openly debate any proposed laws (which are called "bills" until they become laws) before voting either for or against them. If they do not do that or if we do not like the way they vote, we should elect someone else.

What do contracts and laws have to do with truth and lies? Squealer lied to the animals on the farm, and because they did not have written copies of the original rules, they had no proof that the rules had changed. Memory got fuzzy. The animals assumed that Napoleon and Squealer were looking out for the interests of all of the animals. They assumed that Napoleon and Squealer were telling them the truth. As Boxer said, "Napoleon is always right." And the animals believed what they were being told even though it didn't seem quite right.

Part of the art of persuasion is making people believe what you say is true, as Squealer was able to convince the animals. As outsiders, we can clearly see that Squealer is lying his curly little tail off and telling the animals a bunch of lies to get them to do what he wants them to do...as well as to justify the actions of the pigs.

He doesn't just tell little, white lies. He tells whoppers. "Oh, no. You're mistaken. Trading with people has always been allowed." And the animals accept the lies without hardly any question, without holding the pigs to what they (the animals) know in their hearts to be true.

Here are some questions for you to consider to help you draw your own conclusions about these things:

What happens to a society when the people blindly follow their leaders without keeping them honest by questioning their actions and demanding truthful explanations?

Does it matter if leaders are honest or not? If it matters, whose responsibility is it to keep leaders honest and how is it done?

What happens to a society when the people don't pay attention and don't care about what their leaders are doing?

What role does the media play in this issue of truth and lies?

In what ways does the Internet with social media, blogs, and websites empower the people?

Are you honest? Do you believe that people should be honest? Leaders?

What are your own responsibilities as a member of society?

Are you a Boxer? A Molly? A Benjamin? A Snowball?

Why did Napoleon get rid of Snowball and rewrite the history of Snowball's actions?

You're nearing adulthood and looking towards your future and possibly the future of your family, your children, or nieces or nephews. What does any of this mean to you or to them?

VOCABULARY: READING ASSIGNMENT 4
Animal Farm Chapters 9-10

PART I: Using Prior Knowledge And Contextual Clues
Use any clues you can find in the sentences from the text combined with your prior knowledge and write what you think the bold word means.

1. . . . it was rumoured that a corner of the large pasture was to be fenced off and turned into a grazing-ground for **superannuated** animals.

2. There was only one candidate, Napoleon, who was elected **unanimously**.

3. "Up there, comrades," he would say **solemnly**, pointing to the sky with his large beak--"up there, just on the other side of that dark cloud that you can see--there it lies, Sugarcandy Mountain . . . ."

4. They all declared **contemptuously** that his stories about Sugarcandy Mountain were lies . . . .

5. He did not care what happened so long as a good store of stone was accumulated before he went on **pension**.

6. Jones too was dead--he had died in an **inebriates**' home in another part of the country.

7. They accepted everything that they were told about the Rebellion and the principles of Animalism, especially from Clover, for whom they had an almost **filial** respect; but it was doubtful whether they understood very much of it.

8. The source of the trouble appeared to be that Napoleon and Mr. Pilkington had each played an ace of spades **simultaneously**.

Animal Farm Vocabulary: Reading Assignment 4 Page 2

PART II: Matching
Considering the usage in Part I, match the vocabulary words to their definitions.

1. superannuated
2. unanimously
3. solemnly
4. contemptuously
5. pension
6. inebriates
7. filial
8. simultaneously

A. in complete agreement
B. seriously, deeply earnest
C. sum of money paid as a retirement benefit
D. scornfully; with a belittling attitude
E. retired because of age or infirmity
F. drunkards
G. happening at the same time
H. befitting a son or daughter

Part III: Cloze Passage
Fill in the blanks with the appropriate vocabulary words from the list above. You may need to use different forms of the words.

The boss had to make two decisions _____: how to maintain the _____ devotion of his son who worked for him, and how to let him know that he was going to fire him for being an _____. The son's inexcusable, drunken behavior at work and after hours was _____ confirmed by all who worked with him. The boss decided to _____ his son and give him the usual _____. Trying not to deliver his decision _____, the boss _____ informed the young man of his decision.

Animal Farm Vocabulary: Reading Assignment 4 Page 3

PART IV: Words In Practice
Answer the questions and be able to give short explanations to justify your answers.

1. Give an example of the circumstances under which a bus driver might be superannuated.

2. Is it likely that the outcome of a U.S. Presidential election would be by a unanimous decision?

3. In court, witnesses are sometimes asked, "Do you solemnly swear to tell the truth?" What does that mean?

4. Make a facial expression that would be considered contemptuously looking at someone.

5. When do most people start receiving a pension?

6. If someone calls you an inebriate, is that a compliment?

7. Does the word filial have more to do with family relationships or business relationships?

8. When a large group of people in one room all talk simultaneously, is the room likely to be quiet or loud?

PART V:
Below are some other forms of the vocabulary words from Reading Assignment #4.

superannuated - superannuate, superannuates, superannuating
unanimously - unanimous
solemnly - solemn
contemptuously - contemptuous
pension - pensions, pensionless
inebriates - inebriate, inebriated
filial - filially
simultaneously - simultaneous

PART VI: Usage
Write a little story in which you use one form of each of your vocabulary words from Assignment #3.

STUDY QUESTIONS READING ASSIGNMENT 4
Animal Farm Chapters 9-10

1. When rations are "readjusted" Squealer states that "a too rigid equality in rations... would have been contrary to the principles of Animalism." Why does Squealer say this?

2. When Napoleon initially agreed on a contract for eggs, there was a rebellion. Now the contract has been increased to the point where the hens are barely able to maintain their population. Why is there no rebellion now?

3. What is the purpose of the Spontaneous Demonstrations?

4. Why would the pigs permit Moses the Raven to come back?

5. Boxer anticipates several years of rest during his retirement, should he recover after his injury. What actually happens to him?

6. Where do the pigs acquire the money to get the whiskey for Boxer's memorial banquet?

Animal Farm Study Questions Chapters 9-10 Page 2

7. In the final chapter, the windmill is finished at last and the machinery installed. What does it provide the farm animals?

8. What is the truest happiness according to Napoleon? Do you think he believes it? Do you believe it?

9. What is the symbolism of Squealer standing on his hind legs, holding the whip in his trotter?

10. What prevents the animals from protesting the pigs walking on their hind legs?

11. In an allegory, animals and objects are used to represent people. In the final chapter, Mr. Pilkington summarizes the allegory of the book. What does he say?

12. Describe the ending of the book.

13. As *Animal Farm* is a fable, it must have a moral. What is the moral of the story?

EQUALITY, INDIVIDUALITY, and CIVILIZATION
Animal Farm

And, above all, no animal must ever tyrannize over his own kind.
Weak or strong, clever or simple, we are all brothers. No animal
must ever kill any other animal. All animals are equal.

The idea of equality is a noble and desirable one, one we strive for as a society. But, what does it actually mean, and is it possible to achieve?

If you take a pitcher of water and pour it into two identical measuring cups, you can create equal parts. Because the water is the same and the measuring scale is the same, the parts are truly equal. They look the same, they are chemically made up of the same elements, and they are essentially in all aspects identical. But can people be equal?

We each have our own talents, our own characteristics, our own genetics, our own circumstances, our own personalities. A room full of people isn't the same as a pitcher of water. We are not made up of exactly the same elements; we are not identical. Like it or not, some people are gifted with being smart, others are gifted with being artistic, some are gifted with being good at mechanical things or musical things or athletics or caring for others. We are not the same. Some people are good leaders, some people are good persuaders, some people are strong workers: Napoleons, Squealers, or Boxers.

What, then, does it mean to be equal if we are so different? What is the measuring scale we can use to define equality among people?

The key is the second line above: "Weak or strong, clever or simple, we are all brothers." We belong to the brotherhood of mankind. That phrase "the brotherhood of mankind" is loaded with meaning. What do you think it means? If you're thinking it means, "we're all in this world together in the same boat" (so-to-speak), you're right.

Being perfectly politically correct, one would say "the peoplehood of peoplekind" so as not to appear to be sexist, so as not to imply that somehow by using the male version of the phrase that men are somehow superior to women. One major issue in the topic of equality is the equality of men and women, and this is as good of a point to talk about as any other equality issues (for example: equality of races, nationalities, religions).

Are all men and all women equal? Some men are stronger than others; some women are stronger than other women. It's impossible to say, for example, that all men are stronger than all women. So, if there is a job opening that requires a certain amount of strength, would all men be able to do it? No. Would all women? Again, no.

So what is this equality we are striving for in our society? It is the equality of opportunity and the equality of real possibilities. Any man or woman having the requisite strength who applies for the aforementioned job wants the equal opportunity to actually get the job and to receive equal compensation for doing the same work.

We also often hear of "equal housing opportunity." That means when a house or apartment is for sale or for rent, anyone who has the means to pay for the place has an equal opportunity to acquire it without regard to race, religion, nationality, etc.

This is the kind of equality Old Major meant when he said, "All animals are equal." He envisioned a place where the differences among the animals were recognized but each animal still had equal opportunities to contribute and to benefit from the farm. No animals were supposed to be "better" than others; each was to be respected and treated fairly by the others.

The question of whether or not this kind of equality is possible is a central question of the book *Animal Farm*.

Here are some questions to think about related to equality, individualism, and civilization:

1. What is George Orwell's answer to the question of whether or not equality is possible? What evidence is there in *Animal Farm* to support your opinion?

2. Do you think true equality is possible in a society? Why or why not?

3. The Declaration of Independence says, "We hold these truths to be self-evident, that all men are created equal, that they are endowed by their Creator with certain unalienable Rights, that among these are Life, Liberty and the pursuit of Happiness." What does that mean? The Declaration of Independence is a short document. Read it today. You can easily find a copy online for free.

4. If all animals (people) are equal, who makes and enforces laws? What is there to keep people who make and enforce laws (rules) from making unjust rules or too many rules? What ensures the rules are enforced equally and justly?

5. What recourse do people have if they feel they are being unjustly treated in society?

6. Do we live in a civilization in which equality exists? Give examples to support your answer.

Use of Propaganda in *Animal Farm*

Find textual evidence of the use of propaganda in *Animal Farm*. Use the chart below to record your findings.

Chapter & Page	Evidence	Comments/Notes
--		
--		
--		
--		
--		
--		
--		
--		
--		
--		

Use of Propaganda in *Animal Farm*

After you have gathered textual evidence of the use of propaganda in *Animal Farm*, take time to look at this evidence through the whole book.

Here are some questions related to this topic:

1. Where does the propaganda originate?

2. How is the propaganda delivered?

3. What is the purpose of the propaganda?

4. What is the effect of the propaganda?

5. Is the propaganda effective? If so, why does it work?

6. What can you learn from this information?

Steps By Which Pigs Become Human in *Animal Farm*

Find textual evidence of the pigs' becoming like humans in *Animal Farm*. Use the chart below to record your findings.

Chapter & Page	Evidence	Comments/Notes
--		
--		
--		
--		
--		
--		
--		
--		
--		
--		

Steps By Which Pigs Become Human in *Animal Farm*

After you have gathered textual evidence of the steps by which the pigs become more like people in *Animal Farm*, take time to look at this evidence through the whole book.

Here are some questions related to this topic:

1. In what ways do the pigs become more like people?

2. What causes the pigs to become more like people?

3. Is it portrayed as a good or bad thing that the pigs become more like people? Justify your answer.

4. Is it necessary for the pigs to become more like people?

5. How would the story and its themes have been different if the pigs had not become more like people?

Revision of the Commandments in *Animal Farm*

Exactly when and how did the Commandments change in *Animal Farm*. Use the chart below to record your findings.

Chapter & Page	Evidence	Comments/Notes
--		
--		
--		
--		
--		
--		
--		
--		
--		
--		

Revision of the Commandments in *Animal Farm*

After you have gathered textual evidence of how and when the Commandments change in *Animal Farm*, take time to look at this evidence through the whole book.

Here are some questions related to this topic:

1. Who changed the Commandments?

2. Why were the Commandments changed?

3. How were the changes justified or explained to the animals?

4. Did the animals readily accept all the changes to the Commandments? Why or why not?

5. The changes were subtle and done slowly at first. Why?

6. In the end, there is only one Commandment that replaced all the others. What is the last, single Commandment, and what does it mean?

7. What can we learn from studying the changes in the Commandments in the book *Animal Farm*?

Snowball's Fall From Honor in *Animal Farm*

Find textual evidence of Snowball's fall from honor in *Animal Farm*. Use the chart below to record your findings.

Chapter & Page	Evidence	Comments/Notes
--		
--		
--		
--		
--		
--		
--		
--		
--		
--		

Snowball's Fall From Honor in *Animal Farm*

After you have gathered textual evidence of Snowball's fall from honor in *Animal Farm*, take time to look at this evidence through the whole book.

Here are some questions related to this topic:

1. Who was behind turning Snowball from a hero into a villain?

2. Why was Snowball turned into a villain?

3. How was Snowball turned into a villain?

4. Why didn't the animals protect Snowball's reputation and reject the propaganda that rewrote history?

5. What can we learn from studying Snowball's fall from honor in *Animal Farm*?

Man's Inhumanity to Man in *Animal Farm*

Find textual evidence of times Men—or the pigs who become like Men—exhibit what could be considered cruelness to others in *Animal Farm*. Use the chart below to record your findings.

Chapter & Page	Evidence	Comments/Notes
--		
--		
--		
--		
--		
--		
--		
--		
--		
--		

Man's Inhumanity to Man in *Animal Farm*

After you have gathered textual evidence of times Men—or the pigs who become like Men—exhibit what could be considered cruelness to others in *Animal Farm*, take time to look at this evidence through the whole book.

Here are some questions related to this topic:

1. *Inhumanity* means being inhumane; lacking human compassion--being unkind or cruel. What is the difference between exhibiting leadership and being inhumane?

2. List what you think are the three most egregious examples of inhumanity in the novel.

3. What things could cause a person to become inhumane, to act in an cruel or unkind way towards others?

4. What does the word *oppression* mean? Would you consider the animals on Animal Farm to be oppressed? Why or why not?

5. Why is it so hard to have a society in which no one is oppressed? Has it ever been done?

PASSAGES FROM *ANIMAL FARM*

Consider the following passages from *Animal Farm* and explain why each is important.

1. Only get rid of Man, and the produce of our labour would be our own. Almost overnight we could become rich and free....That is my message to you, comrades: Rebellion! (I)

2. Whatever goes upon two legs is an enemy. Whatever goes upon four legs, or has wings, is a friend. And remember also that in fighting against Man, we must not come to resemble him. Even when you have conquered him, do not adopt his vices. No animal must ever live in a house, or sleep in a bed, or wear clothes, or drink alcohol, or smoke tobacco, or touch money, or engage in trade. All the habits of Man are evil. And, above all, no animal must ever tyrannize over his own kind. Weak or strong, clever or simple, we are all brothers. No animal must ever kill any other animal. All animals are equal. (I)

3. He was a brilliant talker, and when he was arguing some difficult point he had a way of skipping from side to side and whisking his tail which was somehow very persuasive. the others said of Squealer that he could turn black into white. (II)

4. . . . .the pigs had succeeded in reducing the principles of Animalism to Seven Commandments. These Seven Commandments would now be inscribed on the wall; they would form an unalterable law by which all the animals on Animal Farm must live forever after. (II)

5. It is for *your* sake that we drink that milk and eat those apples. (III)

6. "I have no wish to take life, not even human life," repeated Boxer, and his eyes were full of tears. (IV)

7. He would be only too happy to let you make your decisions for yourselves. But sometimes you might make the wrong decisions, comrades, and then where should we be? (V)

8. He repeated a number of times, "Tactics, comrades, tactics!" skipping round and whisking his tail with a merry laugh. (V)

9. This work was strictly voluntary, but any animal who absented himself from it would have his rations reduced by half. (VI)

10. From now onwards Animal Farm would engage in trade with the neighbouring farms: not, of course, for any commercial purpose, but simply in order to obtain certain materials which were urgently necessary. (VI)

11. Curiously enough, Clover had not remembered that the Fourth Commandment mentioned sheets; but as it was there on the wall, it must have done so. (VI)

12. Do you know the enemy who has come in the night and overthrown our windmill? SNOWBALL! (VI)

Animal Farm Passages For Discussion Page 2

13. Whenever anything went wrong it became usual to attribute it to Snowball. (VII)

14. Snowball was in league with Jones from the very start! (VII)

15. Did we not see for ourselves how he attempted--fortunately without success--to get us defeated and destroyed at the Battle of the Cowshed? (VII)

16. "Ah, that is different!" said Boxer. "If Comrade Napoleon says it, it must be right." (VII)

17. I do not understand it. I would not have believed that such things could happen on our farm. It must be due to some fault in ourselves. The solution, as I see it, is to work harder. (VII)

18. "It's no longer needed, comrade," said Squealer stiffly. "*Beasts of England* was the song of the Rebellion. But the Rebellion is now completed." (VII)

19. In April, Animal Farm was proclaimed a Republic, and it became necessary to elect a President. There was only one candidate, Napoleon, who was elected unanimously. (IX)

20. ". . . 'Forward in the name of the Rebellion. Long live Animal Farm! Long live Comrade Napoleon! Napoleon is always right.' Those were his very last words, comrades." Here Squealer's demeanour suddenly changed. He fell silent for a moment, and his little eyes darted suspicious glances from side to side before he proceeded. (IX)

21. It was a pig walking on his hind legs. (X)

22. All animals are equal but some animals are more equal than others. (X)

23. "Gentlemen, here is my toast: To the prosperity of The Manor Farm!" (X)

24. The creatures outside looked from pig to man, and from man to pig, and from pig to man again; but already it was impossible to say which was which. (X)

ELEMENTS OF FICTION - CHARACTER TRAITS
Animal Farm

In the small circle, write your character's name. In each larger circle, write one character trait and give an example of that trait from the story. Use as many of the large circles as you need for your character.

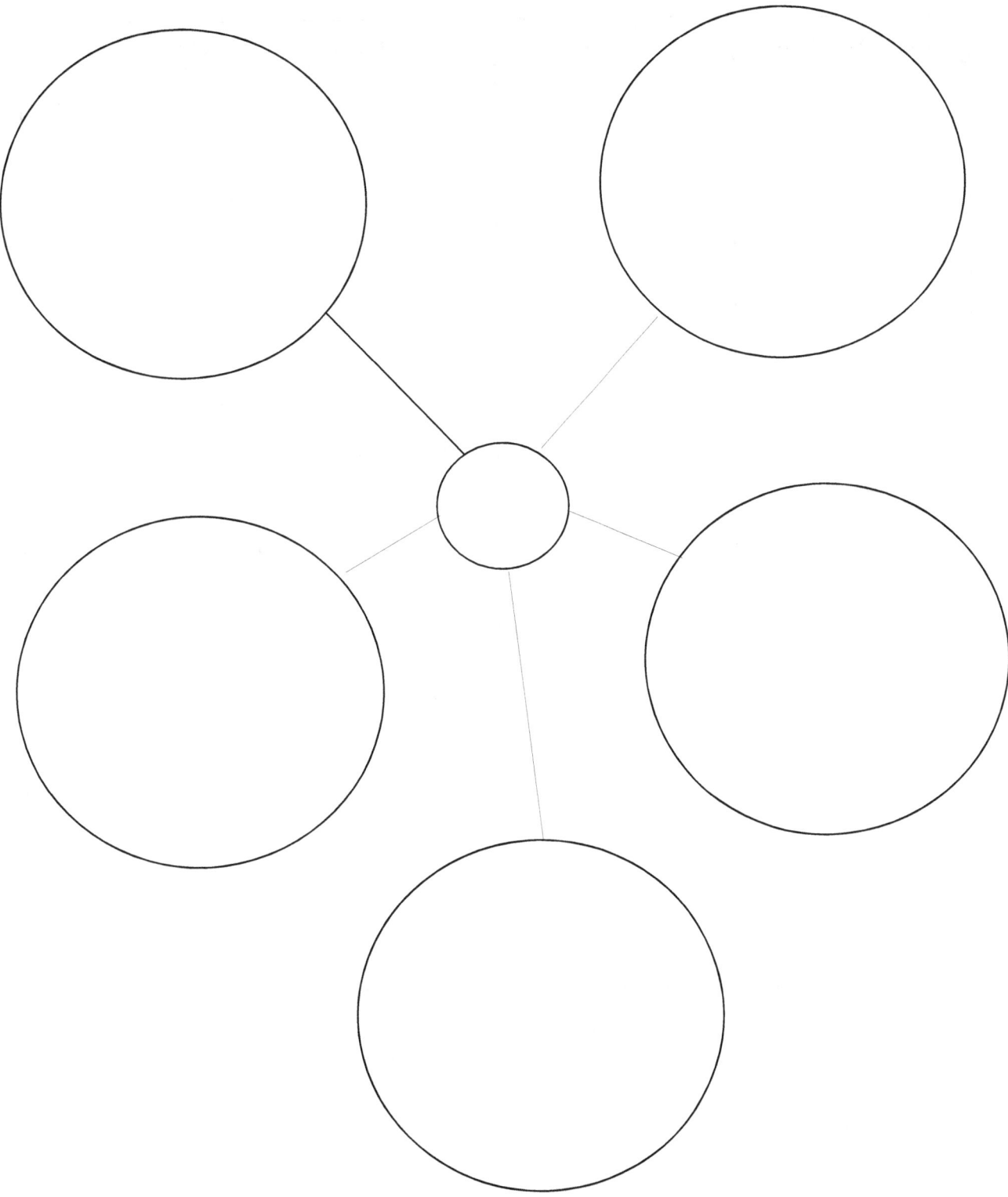

ELEMENTS OF FICTION - CONFLICT CHART
Animal Farm

Under each column, give examples of that type of conflict in *Animal Farm*. Be prepared to explain how the conflict applies in your example.

animal vs. person	animal vs. animal	animal vs. self	animal vs. society

animal vs nature

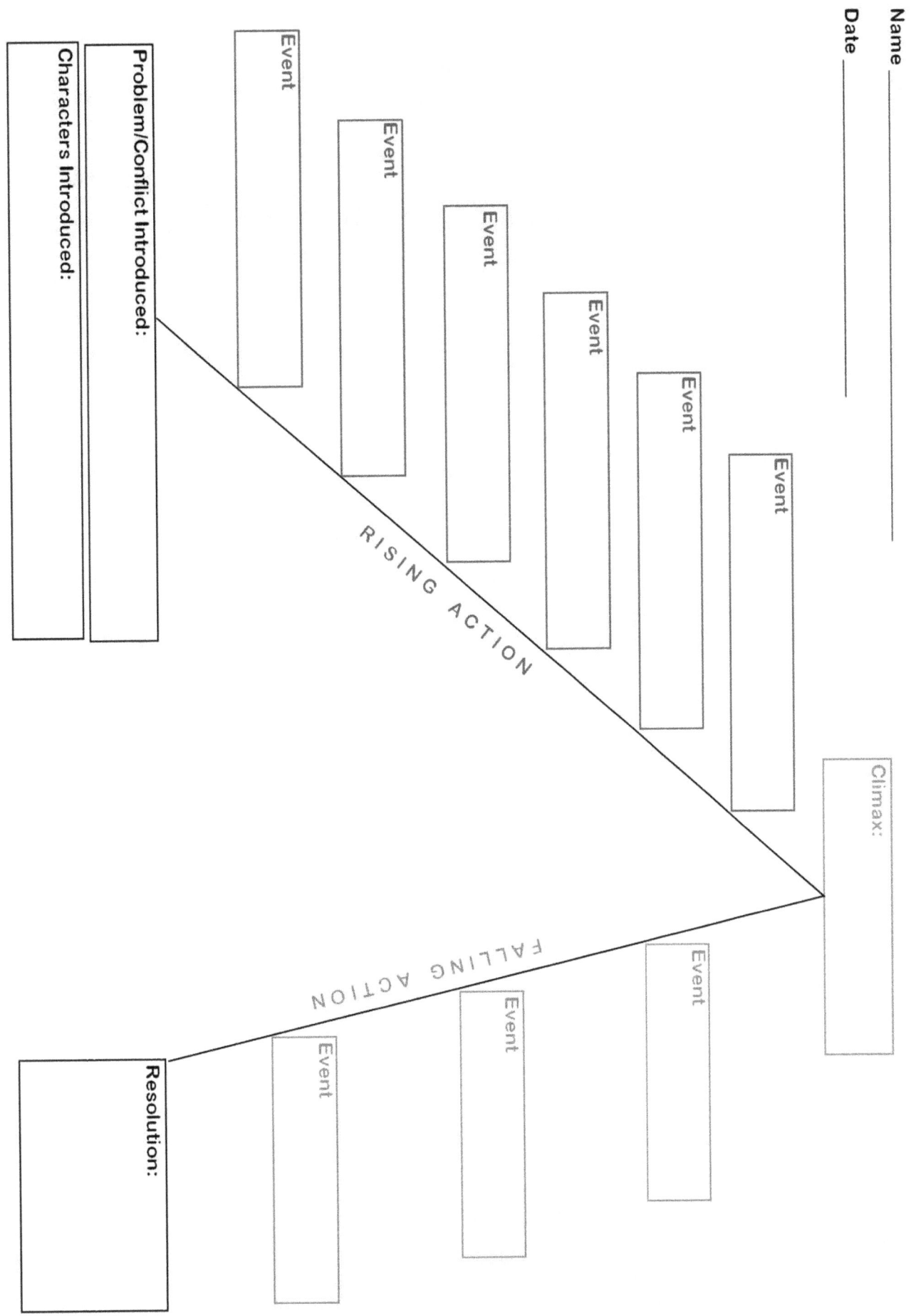

CROSSWORD 1
Animal Farm

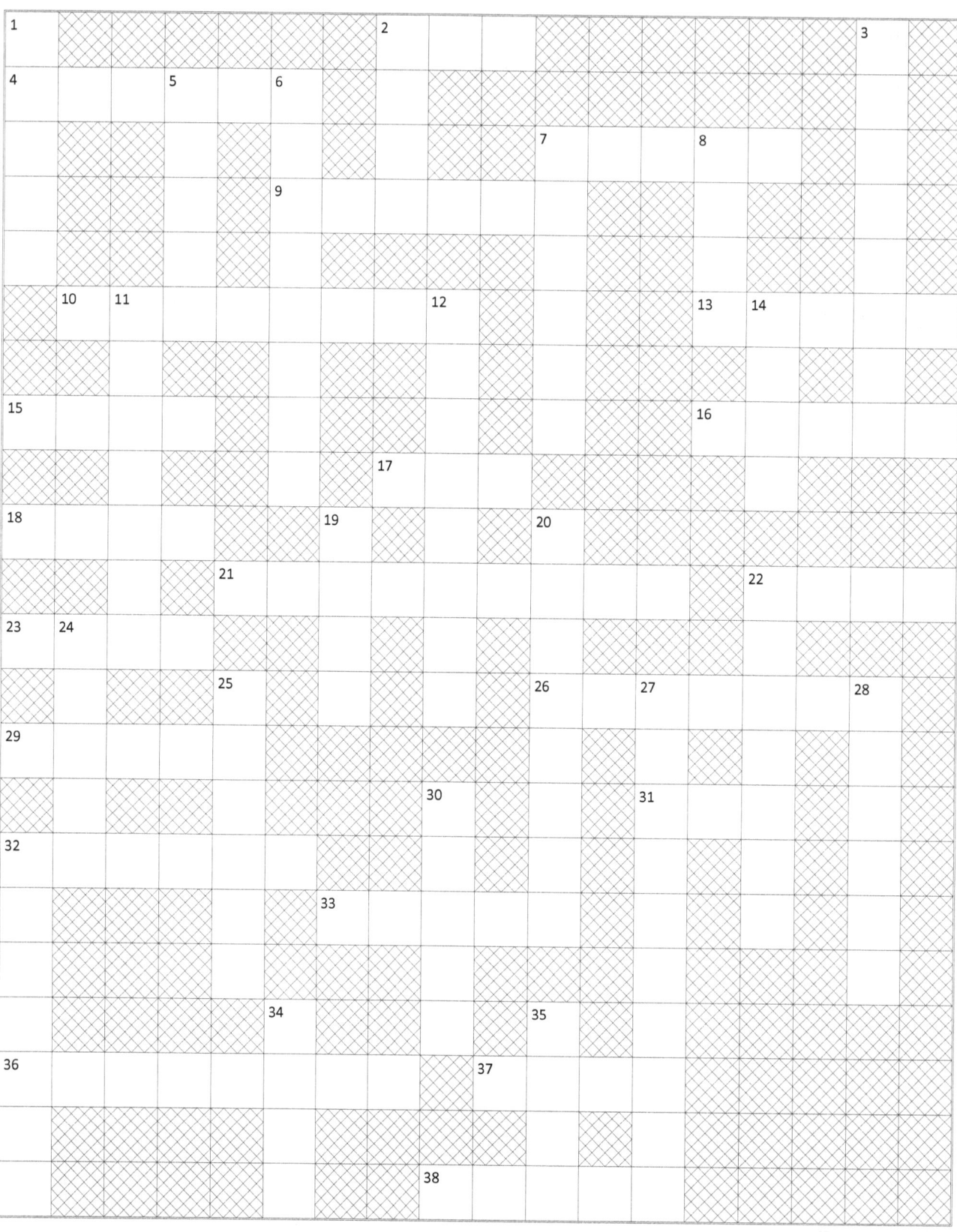

CROSSWORD 1 CLUES
Animal Farm

Across
2. Boxer burns his.
4. The pigs ate these and drank the milk.
7. Huge, strong horse who had two maxims
9. A perfect society
10. Cynical donkey in Animal Farm
13. Animals who are most easily led
15. Napoleon's guard animals
16. The pigs too over Jones's ____.
17. The Battle of the ---shed
18. A material symbol; the animals had a green & white one
21. Efficient neighboring farmer
22. A shortage of it triggered the revolution
23. Pigs began to sleep in these
26. He repeated a number of times, '____, comrades, ___!'
29. Mollie's treat
31. All the habits of ___ are evil.
32. Motherly horse
33. To the prosperity of The ___ Farm!
36. A highly symbolical story with a deeper meaning
37. Boxer: I have no wish to take ___, not even human ____.
38. He told stories about Sugarcandy Mountain.

Down
1. Story in which animals speak & act like humans
2. Snowball was Animal ____, First Class
3. All animals are equal; they are ____.
5. Old Major symbolizes ____.
6. The persuasive pig
7. --- of the Cowshed
8. The hens had to give these up for sale.
11. Beasts of ----
12. Our Leader; the leader of the animals
14. Boxer split his; also the flag had one on it
19. Four ---- good; two --- bad
20. One single ruler with total power
22. Relationship between Boxer and Benjamin
24. All animals are ___, but some are more ____ than others.
25. Author of Animal Farm
27. Decisions were made by ___ of pigs
28. Use of these became forbidden, not the use of beds.
30. Owner of Manor Farm
32. Means *ffriend* or *ffellow worker*
34. Boxer: "I will ___ harder."
35. The cleverest of animals

CROSSWORD 2
Animal Farm

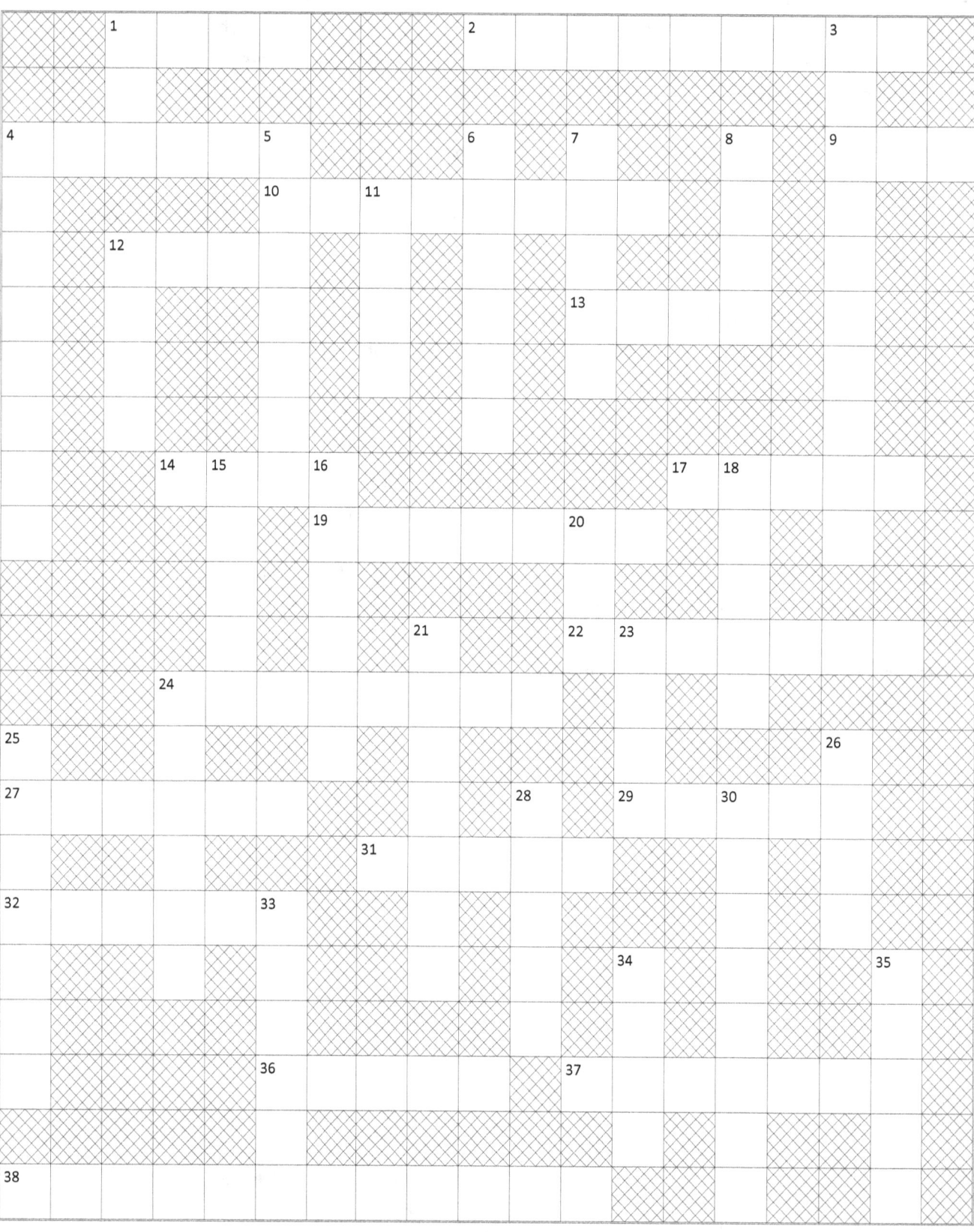

CROSSWORD 2 CLUES
Animal Farm

Across

1. Snowball was Animal ___, First Class
2. Efficient neighboring farmer
4. ___ of the Cowshed
9. All the habits of ___ are evil.
10. Our Leader; the leader of the animals
12. A material symbol of the revolution
13. The hens had to give these up for sale.
14. Pigs began to sleep in these.
17. Animals who are most easily led.
19. He repeated a number of times, "___, comrades, ___!"
22. The pigs drank too much of this at the celebration of Boxer's life.
24. Highly symbolical story with a deeper meaning
27. A perfect society
29. Story in which animals speak & act like humans
31. To the prosperity of the ___ Farm!
32. Use of these became forbidden, not the use of beds.
36. Old Major symbolizes ___.
37. Relationship between Boxer and Benjamin
38. The Seven ___ were written on the end wall of the barn

Down

1. Boxer burns his.
3. Decisions were made by ___ of pigs.
4. Cynical donkey on Animal Farm
5. Beasts of ___
6. Motherly horse
7. Huge, strong horse who had two maxims
8. Napoleon's guard animals
11. The cleverest of animals
12. A shortage of it triggered the revolution.
15. All animals are ___, but some are more ___ than others.
16. Boxer carried tons of these to make the windmill.
18. The pigs took over Jones's ___.
20. The Battle of the ___ shed
21. Means *friend* or *fellow worker*
23. Boxer split his; also the flag had one on it
24. The pigs ate these and drank the milk.
25. Animal Farm is an allegory about the ___ Revolution.
26. Four ___ good; two ___ bad.
28. Owner of Manor Farm
30. All animals are equal; they are ___.
33. Napoleon symbolizes ___.
34. Boxer: "I will ___ harder."
35. He told stories about Sugarcandy Mountain.

VOCABULARY CROSSWORD 1
Animal Farm

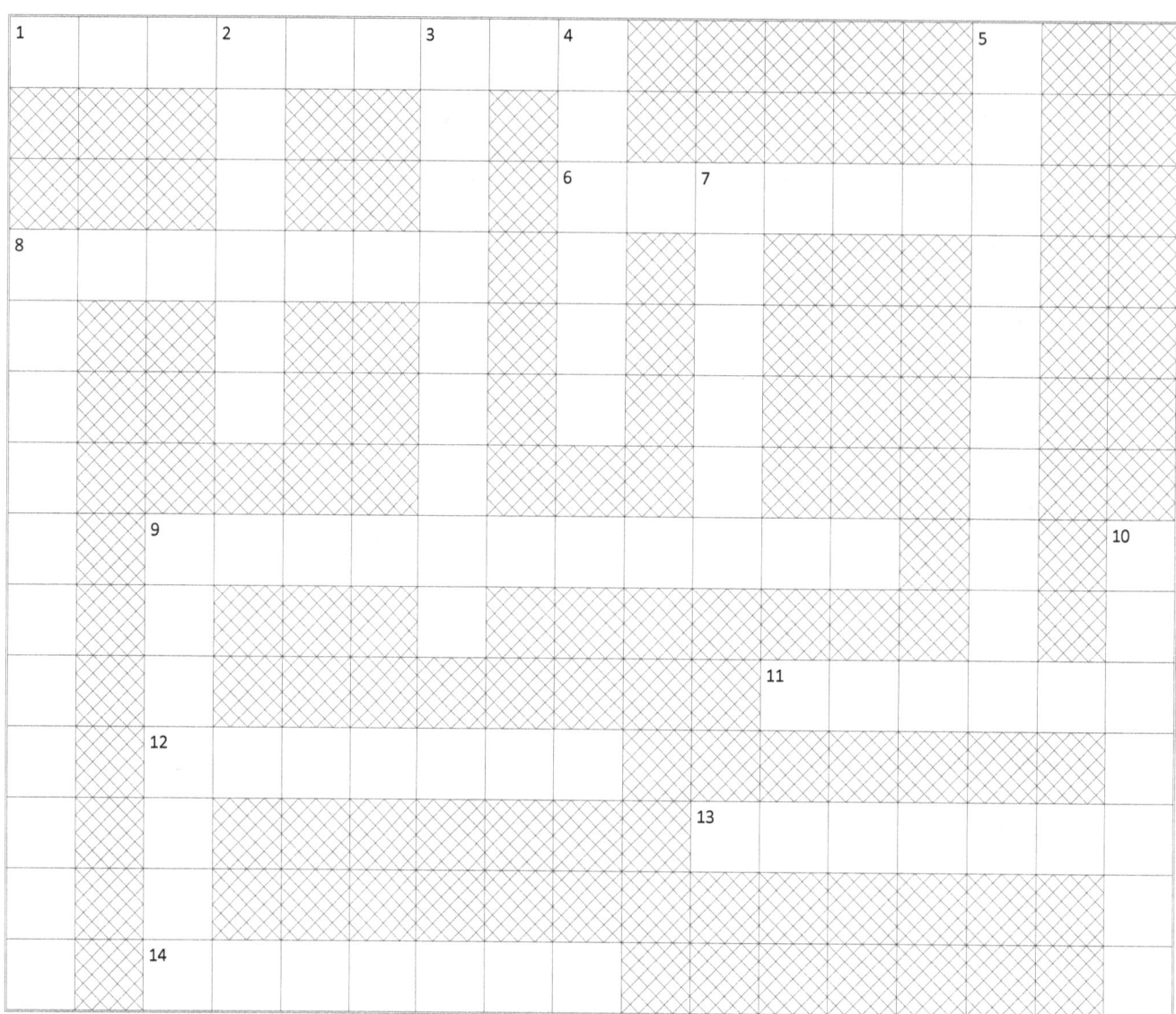

Across
1. Lively; spirited
6. Those accompanying a person of rank
8. Excuse
9. Gave up all resistance
11. Waver in confidence; hesitate; fail
12. Bitterly mocking
13. Sum of money paid as a retirement benefit
14. Exist concealed or unsuspected

Down
2. Lack of interest or emotion
3. Stubbornly inflexible
4. Astute; clever
5. Outstanding
7. Commotion
8. Continually
9. Critical; of supreme importance
10. Absolute power; sep. when used unjustly or cruelly

VOCABULARY CROSSWORD 2
Animal Farm

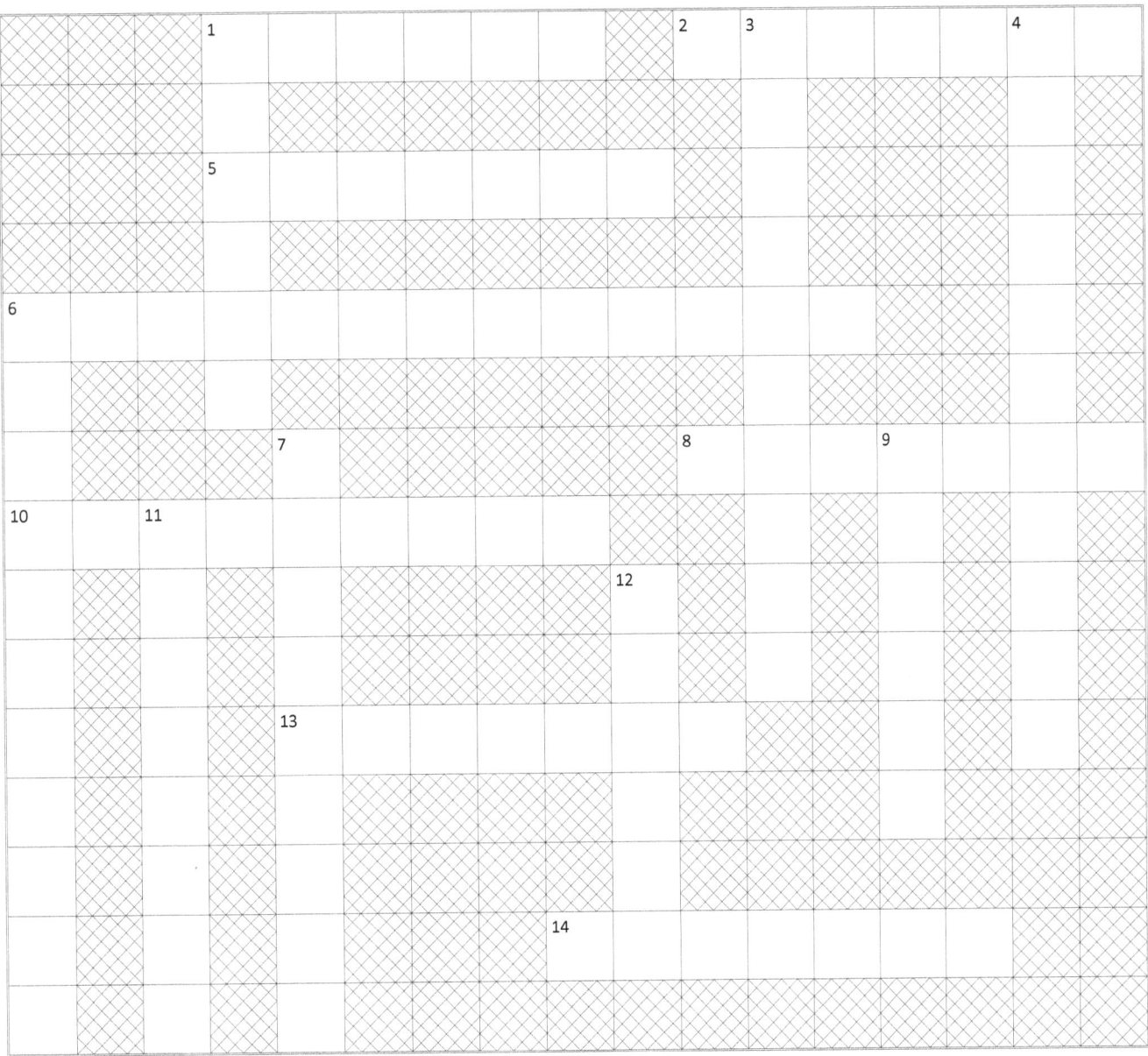

Across
1. Befitting a son or daughter
2. Those accompanying a person of rank
5. Exist concealed or unsuspected
6. Untiring; tireless
8. Sum of money paid as a retirement benefit
10. Stubbornly inflexible
13. Bitterly mocking
14. Absolute power; esp. when used unjustly or cruelly

Down
1. Waver in confidence; hesitate; fail
3. Encouraged; made brave; gave courage to
4. In complete agreement
6. Disgraceful; shameful
7. Lively; spirited
9. Astute; clever
11. Seriously; deeply earnest
12. Lack of interest or emotion

www.ingramcontent.com/pod-product-compliance
Lightning Source LLC
Chambersburg PA
CBHW081502070526
44586CB00019B/2459